Pause and Rewind
in FRANCE

Peter Burgham

Copyright © Peter Burgham 2023

The right of Peter Burgham to be identified as the author of this book has been asserted in accordance with the Copyright, Designs and Patents Act 1988.

First Printing: 2023

ISBN 978-1-9196018-4-7   (paperback)

Published by: Peter Burgham
                 York, England

A CIP catalogue record for this book is available from the British Library.

Website: www.burg34.com

Front Cover: Cannes, south of France

Dedicated to my wife

and our family and friends

with love

PAUSE AND REWIND
in FRANCE

Welcome to this latest in the *Pause and Rewind* series of photo-poems. It's an unusual format, perhaps best described as a hop-on/hop-off tour in light verse. This one focuses on locations in France that I've been fortunate enough to visit over the years. I've tried to include a mixture of urban and rural life, and a variety of poetic styles and moods, so hopefully there is something for everyone.

They can in Cannes
Said a man in Vannes
But in Nantes they can't
Par la plume de ma tante

The cover image shows the bay of Cannes, on the Côte d'Azur. This is perhaps for us Brits the archetypal image of the south of France - sun, sea, yachts, glamour. But there are of course many other facets of French life, and I hope to showcase some of them in the course of this little book. It will however inevitably barely scratch the surface of this amazing country with its richness of history, traditions and unique culture.

In researching the topics, I've travelled to numerous parts of France to explore the territory and sample the local hospitality - ah the many sacrifices I've made for Art !

This collection is a fusion of my own words and photographs. Most of the poems have been newly created for this book, but I've reworked a few from other titles of mine, as they seemed to fit well.

There are several poems written in French. Whilst I speak enough French to get by, you'll be pleased to know that my francophone acquaintances have assisted in refining (ie correcting !) my poetic forays *en français*, so I'm grateful to them. The French poems are not literal translations, but rather they are re-interpretations of the pictures. They are a bonus for French-speakers but easily skipped if you're not.

*

The idea behind *Pause and Rewind* is to take a few moments to reflect on those values and customs which make the world a better place, albeit sometimes they may seem to be in short supply, such as compassion, patience, tolerance and not least a sense of humour. There is much to be grateful for in the part of the world in which we live. Progress doesn't always suit everyone, but we all have the opportunity to shape things for the future, even in a small way, and the next generation carries forward that priceless commodity, hope.

In making the choices of what to include in this short collection, I have inevitably had to omit so many interesting places, but my hope is that at least I may have provided you with a useful taster. *Bon appetit !*

Photo-poems

The idea of **photo-poems** is not new. There are examples from the 19th century, originally evolving from a type of poetry known as 'ekphrastic' in which poems were inspired by works of art. But a modern collection of photo-poems in celebration of the country of France possibly is a first !

The main aim of photo-poetry is to try to combine words with images in an eye-catching way. Ultimately we aspire to create something where the whole seems greater than the sum of the parts. It is true that 'beauty is in the eye of the beholder' and each of you reading/ viewing these pages will form your own opinion, see things in different ways, and that's just fine. But I hope the result in each case will be something positive and satisfying.

we taste the ruby
scent the blue

raise the mainsail
set our course

leave city stripes
behind closed doors

The good news - certainly for me - is that you don't have to be a genius to create a photo-poem. The small example above perhaps illustrates how simple it can be - a snapshot taken on a mobile phone, a little editing with the effects on the computer, and the addition of a few words to try to capture the mood, or react to the picture.

The Image and the Poem, the Places and the People, the Land and the Sea, the one helps to define the other, to see the other in a different light.

So please enjoy these photo-poems and be encouraged to create your own too - be they simple or grandiose, heartfelt or sad, profound or just plain daft !

Peter Burgham

October 2023

Table of Contents

Carcassonne

LOUVRE

a
puzzle
in a prism

safe behind the
glass that's behind
the **door** that's behind
the **glass** that is a **door** that
is a **pyramid** of triangles & steel
bars & rhomboids **wrapped** together
that magnifies the **mystery** and **legend**
of that **enigmatic** **smile** sits the **Mona Lisa**

les vestiges de la Mer de Glace à Montenvers

Disappearing fast
En disparition rapide

the forests and the glacial lakes
coastal towns and kittiwakes
> *les forêts et les lacs glaciaires*
> *toutes les stations balnéaires*

Venice, New Orleans and Jakarta
> *Bangkok, les Maldives et Osaka*

tigers and pandas scarcely found
coral reefs no longer abound
> *les coraux et les tigres chassés*
> *tous les paysages verglacés*

the icebergs and the polar bears
but not alas the billionaires ...
> *les icebergs et les ours polaires*
> *mais hélas pas les milliardaires*

Indicators of global warming are all around us, for example if you look at old photos of glaciers and compare them to modern views taken at the same time of year. A century ago the 'sea of ice' Montenvers glacier in Haute-Savoie (pictured above in 2022) filled the valley, and even 30 years ago it had significantly more depth than today. It is rapidly declining and has become a symbol of the impact of climate change. Man-made problems may well have man-made solutions, but time is not on our side ...

The sun explodes onto the beach
Seagulls shriek staccato shells
Blood rots beneath the pounded sand

But no thunder claims the sky today
Dunkerque reste seule et reposée
She is at ease with the waves

Tranquillité

Dunkirk beac

If William McGonagall had visited Avignon

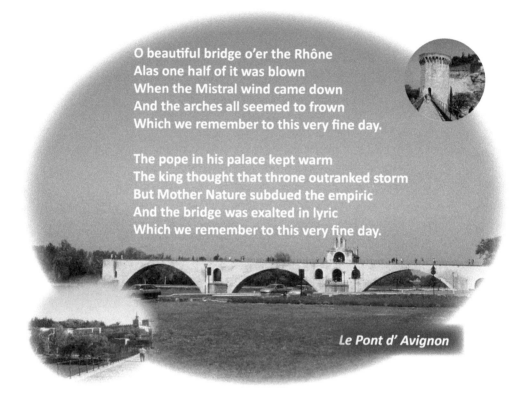

O beautiful bridge o'er the Rhône
Alas one half of it was blown
When the Mistral wind came down
And the arches all seemed to frown
Which we remember to this very fine day.

The pope in his palace kept warm
The king thought that throne outranked storm
But Mother Nature subdued the empiric
And the bridge was exalted in lyric
Which we remember to this very fine day.

Le Pont d' Avignon

Sur le Pont d'Avignon
L'on y danse, l'on y danse ...

With acknowledgement to William McGonagall's memorable poem 'The Tay Bridge Disaster'.

This amazing tree sculpture *Arbre multicolore* (multi-coloured tree) by Philippe Million is located on the plaza of Châteaucreux station along with other *objets d'art*, such as the *Sièges tabourets* (stud seats) in the centre foreground, by François Bauchet, and the *Chevaux bleus* (blue horses) by Assan Smati, far left background.

Photo: September 2007

Illuminations

In the Sixties this is how they envisaged future cityscapes.

They sketched a solar-powered lamppost swarmed by thousands of glass butterflies.

They imagined a bouquet of rainbow paints being pulled from a hat.

They dreamt of luminous birds nesting.

Châteaucreux

Un arc-en-ciel brisé en mille éclats, gemmes étincelantes, un kaléidoscope

de plexiglass et d'acier, feu de joie sur monochrome.

Faux-semblant, un accroche-regard qui offre au voyageur

un moment insolite à suspendre le parcours terne et gris.

Channelling

It might be the rig-chords
strummed by the breeze, the flutter
of a flag, a jangle of keys, a snatch of talk
at a marina bar, the furl of a sail, the cut of a spar,
the horn of a moped on the bustling quay, the shimmering
reflections of the circus-mirror sea, the amber moonlight on the
harbour wall, a champagne fizz,
or nothing at all ...

Antibes, 2023

The old port was the heart of Antipolis, the original
Greek colony on the Côte d'Azur now known as Antibes.
In its modern iteration, Antibes has the largest yacht
marina in Europe. It is a longtime favourite of artists
(Monet, Renoir, Picasso), writers (Hemingway, F. Scott
Fitzgerald, Graham Greene) and royalty (Queen Victoria,
Tsar Alexander II). A place of romance.

Le bon vieux temps

C'était le bon temps.
Les yachts, le soleil ambre
couchant, le vent qui gratte
les gréements comme
des cordes de guitare.

Flânant le long du quai,
nous hissons des drapeaux,
estimons nos chances
de tomber ensemble
dans la mer miroitée.

Ces jours où
tu pouvais y arriver,
c'était le bon temps.

L'Aiguille du Midi

Araignées du ciel
suspendues
au-dessus des glaciers
tissent leurs toiles
à jamais immortalisées

A team of 30 or so mountaineers (nicknamed 'spidermen' locally) each carrying a 30kg backpack of cable tackled the ascent of the Aiguille du Midi in 1949 to establish the initial trial of the longest suspended cable in the world, the forerunner of the cablecar system that still runs today.

Chamonix

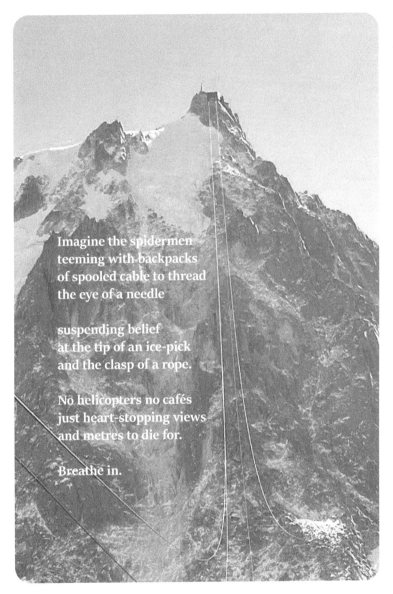

Imagine the spidermen
teeming with backpacks
of spooled cable to thread
the eye of a needle

suspending belief
at the tip of an ice-pick
and the clasp of a rope.

No helicopters no cafés
just heart-stopping views
and metres to die for.

Breathe in.

Remembrance in Northern France
World War I

I made a tour of the WWI battlefields of northern France in 2022 to visit museums, monuments and historic locations in remembrance of those who took part in that terrible conflict.

Arras

Somme

Lille

Armentières

Albert

Nous nous souviendrons d'eux

Keen as mustard, fervent young men,
tanked up on reels of glory, angel-faced,
with dandy suits and dandy boots out they stepped,
the fireworks whizzed, the noise never stopped,
and they cheered like it was 1899 all over again.

They twisted and danced like crazy loons,
threw silver balls and ran and chased,
bathed in the mud springs then slid down
the hall and sang a last song at the break of dawn
as the pipers played their peerless tunes.

Saint-Cézaire-sur-Siagne
hilltop village in *Alpes-Maritimes*
near *Grasse*, pictured in August 2016

Ce qui est essentiel

*À la mémoire de la Libération
ces petits drapeaux graciles
alliés tous en l'honneur
- le sentier mortel si fragile -
du courage, de l'esprit, et du cœur.*

THIS IS WHAT IT TAKES

Against the odds and yet they came
hanging tough to make the climb
through mortar shots and smoke of battle
an anvil for a hammer so brittle
stubborn and brave they held their course
and damned the devil to the cross.

Now breezy flags adorn the town
where once all hope was flying thin
an air salute lest we forget
the daring, the spirit, the goddam grit.

In August 1944, as part of Operation Dragoon, the occupied village of *Saint-Cézaire-sur-Siagne* was liberated by allied forces notably the US First Airborne Task Force.

Languedoc hospitality

In **Bordeaux** *escargots* with *huitres* and wine
- just like a Saturday night in **Newcastle-upon-Tyne**

In **Nice** they love *écrevisses* and *salade niçoise*
- in **Glasgow** they're nae slow with the deep-fried Mars bars

In **Lyon** today it's *quenelles de brochet* and no hurry
- but it's in and out quick in **Brum** with a vindaloo curry

In **Lille** the deal is good beers and waffles
- same as in **Salford** but skipping the waffles

In **Besançon** the *saumon* and *raclette* tempt their lips
- while up north in **Blackpool** it's all fish 'n' chips

In **Paris** they swear by *grenouilles* and *crabes*
- think jellied eels in **London**, or donner kebab

It's true that in **France** they have such different ways
- in **Britain** we'll just stick to our age-old *clichés*.

For us Brits, it is the weather which is our inevitable topic of conversation, but for *les Français* it is undoubtedly *la gastronomie*.

Here's some rather unlikely examples of gastronomical twin towns.

Les Ch'tis *

Les frites fortes se ramassent à la pelle
Les gens du nord les emportent
Dans la nuit froide, sans oublier le sel

[Avec reconnaissance à Jacques Prévert
et son poème <<Les feuilles mortes>> .]

* Northerners

16

You've stolen my heart
it's the perfect crime

it's no exaggeration
for you I'd do the time

in your *cagole* arms
with the accent on

sunshine and pleasure

bah ouais ma chère
I'll always treasure
your *pastaga* and your
bouillabaisse

because

for all your swagger
and your fancy talk

assurément

there is no better place
    no Bordeaux charm
    no Paris chic

you're beyond them all
tu es magnifique.

Cliché de ma belle Marseille

Marseille pictured from *La Gare de Saint Charles* in July 2023

*Tu as volé mon cœur
c'est un crime parfait*

*ton sourire attirant
met l'accent sur
nos tête-à-têtes*

*avec tes charmes de
cagole
et tes paroles
tarpin drôles
vos murs bien colorés*

tè vé

*les bandits et les voyous
peu importe
je m'en fiche
d'une telle sorte*

on craint dégun

*et voilà ma déclaration
avec peu d'exagération*

*trente-six mille fois
je te tiens au cœur*

*je t'aime, je t'aime
ma jolie fleur*

Marseille is France's second city, and officially the sunniest, for centuries a cosmopolitan crossroads of trade and immigration. Its most famous street is *la Canebière* leading down to *le Vieux Port*. Overlooking the port on a hilltop is the *Basilique Notre-Dame-de-la-Garde*, also warmly referred to as *la Bonne Mère* by the local people - whose sing-song accent is also often warmly referred to !

Chanson d'Amour

It would have been so easy
to miss you, unassuming
amongst the loud canvases
of all the Eiffel Towers
Louvres and Montmartres
a ray of light in an attic
a single rose
in a secret garden
ma belle dame de Paris
my fabric and my frame.

Rive Gauche

Le chancre coloré

le bleu d'Azur
l'écorce argentée
le chant qui tombe
des feuilles vertes
mais toi toujours
à l'ombre

Cours Mirabeau in Aix-en-Provence

The famous and venerable *platanes* on the *Cours Mirabeau* and elsewhere in *Aix* were blighted by a canker stain (*chancre coloré*) in 2016. Many have subsequently had to be felled and replaced.

A similar fate awaited almost half of the many thousands of *platanes* along the banks of the *Canal du Midi*, a UNESCO World Heritage Site, where diligent replanting is also now under way.

Tomorrow

Though days are wafer-thin
The sky will weave its azure silk.

Though shadows haunt the hours
The emerald crown invites the sun.

Though roots are canker-wracked
The silver bark defies its pain.

When days turn sylvan black
The Earth will spin and hope.

Les arrosoirs arrosés
('watering-cans watered')
by Bertrand Lavier
seen in Montpellier 2022

Left alone we're humble
Together we are proud
Solo we may grumble
But ensemble sing out loud
On our own we'll stumble
But united we're unbowed
We make artwork from a jumble
To stand out from the crowd

Le flair
français

Unknown title (Les planèteurs ... ?)
(mine : 'plantpots spotted')
Unknown artist
seen in Tuileries, Paris 2007

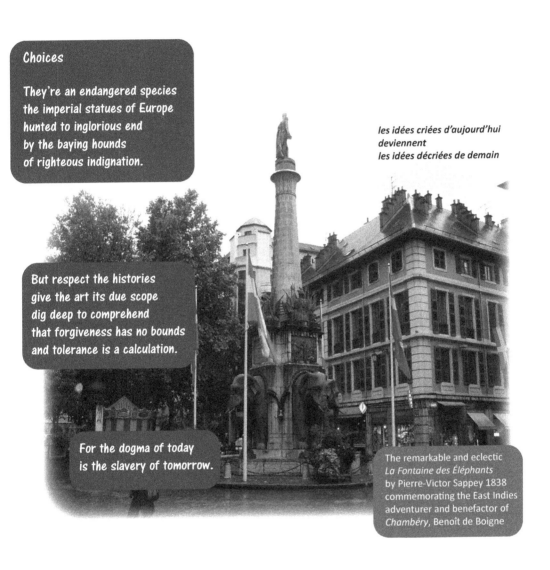

Choices

They're an endangered species
the imperial statues of Europe
hunted to inglorious end
by the baying hounds
of righteous indignation.

*les idées criées d'aujourd'hui
deviennent
les idées décriées de demain*

But respect the histories
give the art its due scope
dig deep to comprehend
that forgiveness has no bounds
and tolerance is a calculation.

For the dogma of today
is the slavery of tomorrow.

The remarkable and eclectic
La Fontaine des Éléphants
by Pierre-Victor Sappey 1838
commemorating the East Indies
adventurer and benefactor of
Chambéry, Benoît de Boigne

Chambéry

21

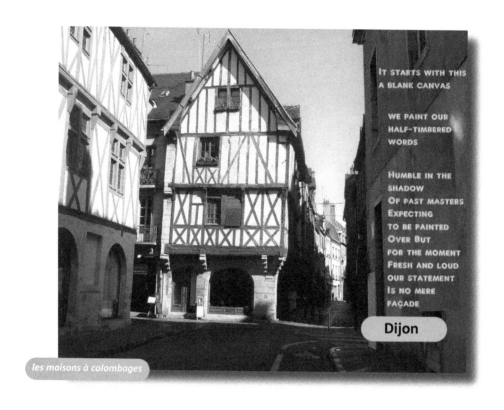

les maisons à colombages

IT STARTS WITH THIS
A BLANK CANVAS

WE PAINT OUR
HALF-TIMBERED
WORDS

HUMBLE IN THE
SHADOW
OF PAST MASTERS
EXPECTING
TO BE PAINTED
OVER BUT
FOR THE MOMENT
FRESH AND LOUD
OUR STATEMENT
IS NO MERE
FAÇADE

Dijon

It starts with this, a blank canvas.
We paint our half-timbered words
humble in the shadow of past masters
expecting to be painted over but
for the moment fresh and loud
our statement is no mere façade.

Montpellier

Street Art Sketch

They cross the lines
They reshape the box
They make us rewire
The orthodox.

They bring us an edge
They get to the nub
Behind the mask
We're all one club.

Dans quel monde Vuitton ?

Le pouvoir des pochoirs
Anime les rues
Fait vivre l'espoir
Toutes saisons confondues

Avec reconnaissance
à l'artiste EZK

Trompe-l'oeil mural at *Place Édouard Adam, Montpellier*, created by *Agnès et Olivier Costa (Mad'Art Concept)* in 2005

You may have heard :
Street artists handle criticism well, they just brush it off ... There was this one artist who was so good she drew a crowd ... Then there was the artist who was arrested but claimed he'd been framed ...
Aaargh, enough ! I draw the line ...

Breizh
Brittany
Bretagne

How glorious
the noisy
hydrangeas in
this awkward
little corner
of the field
confounding
the prim ranks
of bossy lilies.

Quimper en Finistère, Bretagne

grainy old photos taken during
my tour of Brittany in the 1970s

The *Breton* language was banned in French schools until the early
1950s. There was a resurgence of interest in preserving and
developing the language, culture, and music in the 1970s. A *Breton*
couple eventually won their court case to include a non-standard
tilde   in the name of their son. But the struggle against conformity
continues into the 21st century…
… and alas the *Breizh* language is yet another endangered species.

Ur yezh hepken n'eo ket a-walc'h
One language is not enough
Une seule langue ne suffit pas

TGV - à toute vitesse

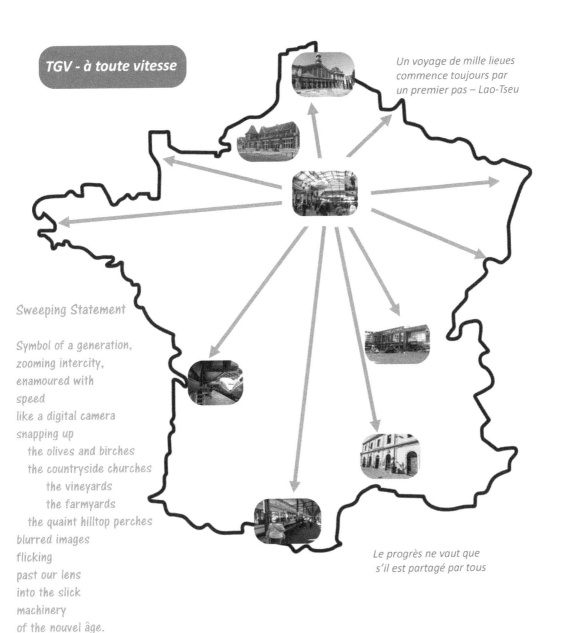

*Un voyage de mille lieues
commence toujours par
un premier pas – Lao-Tseu*

Sweeping Statement

Symbol of a generation,
zooming intercity,
enamoured with
speed
like a digital camera
snapping up
 the olives and birches
 the countryside churches
 the vineyards
 the farmyards
 the quaint hilltop perches
blurred images
flicking
past our lens
into the slick
machinery
of the nouvel âge.

*Le progrès ne vaut que
s'il est partagé par tous*

*Ce n'est pas le voyage que vous faites
c'est le voyage qui vous fait*

Launched over 40 years ago, the TGV high-speed train changed perceptions of rail travel in France. The network has extended, but it remains noticeably Paris-centric. By definition the TGV gets you to long-distance destinations rapidly, but it does thunder past a lot of very interesting places along the way …

Prenez soin de vous

Target for the day

Keep it fresh

5

Keep it real

Stay local

Stay together

WAZEMMES MARKET IN LILLE

ACKNOWLEDGEMENTS

Poems similar to previously published ones in the **Pause and Rewind** series, but reworked here:

Disappearing Fast	*(new bilingual version)*
Châteaucreux	*(French translation of the original)*
Pyramid at The Louvre	*(new version)*

Previously published in **Bird's Eye View**:

Keen as Mustard	*(modified extract from 'Lamplight 1916')*

Previously published in **Creative Juices** *(Ripon Poetry Anthology 2023)*:

Tomorrow	*(published as 'Cancer Ward')*

Other Collections by the same author:

BIRD'S EYE VIEW
(anthology including several prize-winning and commended poems,
 recommended by New Writing North, Sept 2021)

TRIBUTE NIGHT AT THE SOCIAL
(3rd prize, Yeovil Writing Without Restrictions Competition, 2017)

WHISPER ON THE SHORE

TOUCHPOINTS

PAUSE AND REWIND
(series of photo-poems)

More poetry and verse and links to other creative arts can be found on:

www.burg34.com

Disclaimer: There is no unequivocal endorsement or any criticism implied with regards anywhere, anything or anyone mentioned in this book.

Printed in the USA
CPSIA information can be obtained
at www.ICGtesting.com
CBHW041648191023
1413CB00017B/196

9 781919 601847